OPERATION ORCHARD

ISRAELI MOSSAD

ISRAEL'S STRIKE ON THE
SYRIAN REACTOR

DAN MAGEN

Operation Orchard
Israel's Strike On The Syrian Reactor

TABLE OF CONTENTS

INTRODUCTION

I want to thank you and congratulate you for buying this book, "Operation Orchard - Israel's Strike On The Syrian Reactor."

Operation Orchard was an alleged risky airstrike conducted by Israel on a suspected nuclear reactor site in Syria (Deir ez-Zor region) on September 6, 2007 a little after midnight. For 7 months, both the US and Israeli governments imposed blackouts on all new reports about the raid.

Subsequently, the Central Intelligence Unit (CIA), and the White House confirmed that American intelligence had confirmed that the raided site was a military purpose nuclear facility. Syria denied those claims.

In 2009, an investigation conducted by the IAEA (International Atomic Energy Agency) reported traces of graphite and uranium and concluded that the raided site had features resembling an undeclared nuclear reactor.

However, IAEA could not confirm or deny the findings because Syria had refused to provide IAFA investigators the co-operation they needed to take their investigations to a conclusive end. On

April 2011, almost four years after the raid, IAEA officially confirmed that the bombed site was indeed a nuclear reactor.

How did it happen? What weren't we told? To know more about this operation, this is the right book for you. You will learn everything you need to know about the Operation Orchard. Thanks again for downloading this book. I hope you enjoy it!

BEFORE THE AIRSTRIKE: THE ISRAEL AND SYRIA CONFLICT

Israel is a country known to have a number of enemies. Mostly, this conclusion is an apt one especially when you consider the fact that Israel is a Jewish country surrounded by Arab countries. Among the countries that surround Israel is Syria, a country that since the establishment of the State of Israel, has been in constant war with Israel.

These two countries have fought three main wars, including the six-day war in 1967, the Yom Kippur War in 1973, and the ArabIsraeli war of 1948. The two countries also participated in the Lebanon war of 1982.

At some points in this obvious rivalry, the State of Israel and the Syrian Arab Republic signed armistice arrangements or formal agreement between parties at war to stop fighting. Although these neighboring countries have signed these agreements, most have been unsuccessful.

In fact, Syria does not recognize the State of Israel and does not allow holders of Israeli passports to enter into Syria. Israel also regards Syria as an enemy and prohibits any of its citizens from going there.

Since the creation of both countries, there has not been any diplomatic relations between them. There are also no cultural or economic ties between the two countries and only a limited number of people move across the border. Syria also continues to be part of the Arab League Boycott of Israel (a collective Arab member states boycott aimed at preventing Arab countries from trading with Israel to avoid adding to its military and economic strength).

Israel Becomes Suspicious

As you can tell by now, Syria and Israel are out rightly self-proclaimed enemies. This has caused Israel, militarily superior to Syria, to watch every action conducted in or by Syria with a keen eye including the 2001 induction of president Bashar al-Assad.

Israel's Mossad (meaning the institute") is a shortened name for HaMossad leModi in uleTafkidim Meyuh adim, a name that means 'Institute for Intelligence and Special Operations' is one of the major entities in Israel's external intelligence services.

The entity is responsible for counterterrorism, covert operations, intelligence collection, and protecting Jewish communities. The director of Mossad answers directly to the Prime minister of Israel.

Mossad began profiling president Bashar al-Asaad of Syria after North Korean dignitaries visited Syria with the topic of discussion being the delivery of arms.

Israel's military intelligence (Aman) suggested that the topic of discussions was equipping Syria with nuclear arms even though Syria was a signatory of the Treaty on the Non-Proliferation of Nuclear weapons, however, Mossad dismissed the theory.

The Non-Proliferation of Nuclear weapons treaty, commonly called the NPT, is an international treaty used to prevent the spread of nuclear weapon technology and nuclear weapons in general. The treaty promotes nuclear energy cooperation, the peaceful use of nuclear energy, and nuclear disarmament should the need arise.

During the spring of 2004, the United States Intelligence reported multiple communications between North Korea and Syria. The back and forth calls traced back to a desert in Syria called al-Kibar a desert-like location in a remote area of the North Eastern Syria, near the Euphrates River and the border of Iraq. This made unit 8200, Israel's signals intelligence and code breaking unit, to add that location to its watch list.

On 22 April 2004, a huge explosion happened on a North Korean freight train headed to the port of Namp'o. The explosion was so enormous that it registered a magnitude of 3.6 on a Richter scale, a magnitude equivalent to that of a small earthquake. The explosion led to the deaths of several hundreds of people, destroyed a town, and left 2,000 people wounded.

According to the government of North Korea, the train was ferrying liquefied petroleum, a claim that became impossible to verify once the regime banned any further reporting about the incident. One week later, North Korea imposed a 5-year ban on the use of cell phones. This meant no communication about what had happened in the country would reach the outside world. Israel, however, keenly followed this incident.

Aluf Meir Dagan, then Israel's top spy and chief of Mossad, was a brutal man who would do anything to secure Israel's national security. Despite the fact that North Korea was secretive about what they usually do, this case was different. After he received intelligence reports about a Syrian military plane that had landed in North Korea, Dagan grew suspicious especially.

The plane was supposed to be delivering aid for the explosion but instead, intelligence reports indicated that the plane was ferrying away bodies of the people who died in the explosion. What was more suspicious was that before transportation, the Syrians placed the dead bodies in lead lined coffins. Further, people who were wearing chemical weapon suits were responsible for the ferry. ing the bodies, which made the incident extremely strange.

Dagan then received more intelligence reports informing him the bodies were not of North Koreans, the bodies were of Syrian scientists. According to the reports, the bodies were those of 12 Syr. ian scientists who had come from the Syrian Scientific Research Centre, a covert military research and acquisition center.

Mossad also came to learn that a number of Syrian nuclear technicians were in one of the compartments of the train that had exploded. They had arrived in North Korea to collect fissionable material stored in a sealed wagon in the train.

The North Korean regime had also cordoned a wide area around the explosion site for a couple of days. North Korean Soldiers wearing anti-contamination suits sprayed the area and collected the wreckage. Analysts at Mossad suspected North Korea was trying to recover weapon-grade plutonium from the scene. This raised the possibility that North Korea was helping Syria build a nuclear bomb.

Evidence Gathering

In December 2006, approximately 2 years after the explosion, a woman arrived at a hotel bar in London, and a man who was drinking alone noticed her. What the man did not know was that the meeting was a setup. The man was a ranking Syrian nuclear official who had traveled to London for a meeting, and the woman was a Mossad agent sent to distract him. The man had used a false name to check into the London hotel. Mossad had detected the booking at the London hotel and dispatched 10 undercover agents.

The agents are divided into 3 groups. One group camped at Heathrow Airport to identify the Syrian official upon arrival. The second group booked rooms at the hotel and the third one was to 'tail' him and monitor all his movements and visitors. Some of the agents were from the Israeli Kidon Division, a division that specializes in assassinations, and the other were from the Neviot division, a division that specializes in breaking into hotel rooms, homes, and embassies and installing bugging devices.

At the bar, unaware he was under surveillance, the man started flirting with the woman. The woman's mission was to keep the Syrian official busy as the team from the Neviot division broke into his hotel room.

It took the Neviot team seconds to override the hotel's security. Once inside, they were lucky enough to find the official's laptop completely unguarded. They then copied the contents of the lap. top's hard drive and transferred the data to Mossad's Headquarters located in Tel Aviv.

They also installed software that allowed Mossad to monitor all future activities on the laptop. After successfully completing their mission, they all left including the female Mossad agent who was distracting the Syrian at the bar.

Approximately 15 minutes later at Mossad's headquarters in Tel Aviv, analysts started analyzing the contents of the laptop. What they found was rather extraordinary. On one of the folders, they found an image of a North Korean nuclear official known as Chon Chibu meeting with Syria's atomic energy director, Ibrahim Othman. The images looked older, as if taken some years ago.

The analysts also analyzed hundreds of photos documenting the building of a large industrial facility (about 130ft by 130ft and 70ft tall). Initially, they were not sure what the facility in the photos was, but later realized what it was after spotting large industrial equipment inside the facility.

The building was an exact replica of something Dagan had seen before. It resembled images of another nuclear facility in North Korea, the Yongbyon Nuclear research centre. The reactor in the images was an exact replica of the one in the North Korean nu. clear facility. At this point, there was no doubt about the information they had uncovered. This was evidence that North Korea was building a nuclear reactor in Syria.

Although Mossad had planned to kill the official in London, they later decided to spare him following the new discoveries they had uncovered from the contents of his laptop.

Generally, the existence of a nuclear weapon program in Syria is a direct threat to Israel's national security, a threat that called for immediate neutralization because whoever was in charge of building the nuclear reactor had a purpose of building a nuclear bomb.

At this point, Dagan, the chief of Mossad, had evidence there was a nuclear weapons program in Syria; however, he did not know the exact location of the building. He ordered Israeli satellites to monitor potential areas and finally, he pinpointed al-Kibar. This area had an unusual spike of telephone communique with North Korea. Israeli satellites also pinpointed the exact building based on its similarities to the images obtained from the official's laptop.

With the new information on the Syrian facility, Dagan notified Ehud Olmert, the Israeli Prime Minister. The prime minister immediately acknowledged the threat. Together, they determined that the only way to neutralize the threat was through an air strike that would blow up the reactor.

The next month, the Israeli Prime Minister formed a panel of three members to report on the nuclear program undertaken by Syria. Six months later, one of the panel members, General Yaakov Amidror, informed the prime minister that Syria was working with Iran and North Korea on the nuclear facility.

Iran had channeled $1 billion to the project. Iran had also planned to use the Kibar facility to replace the Iranian facilities if it was unable to finish its Uranium enrichment program.

In July 2007, an explosion happened at Musalmiya area in Northern Syria; the explosion injured 50 people and killed 15 Syrian military personnel. Reports indicated that 'very explosive materials' blew up in the facility after a fire broke out. However, in September the same year, reports indicated the explosion occurred after a failed attempt to use Mustard gas to weaponize a Scud C missile. This incident also made Israel more suspicious of what was going on in Syria.

In early summer 2007, a senior U.S official told ABC News that Mossad had successfully inserted a spy who posed as an employee who would co-opt one of the workers in the facility to take pictures of the target from the ground. Later, Israel launched a spy satellite into space (Ofek-7). This Israel geo positioned the satellite in a way that allowed them to use it to watch activity at the Syrian nuclear reactor complex.

However, before they could launch an attack, they needed to know how far advanced the reactor was at that time. The need to do this came from the fact that if the reactor was operational, it would cause an enormous environmental pollution-poisoning catastrophe.

Mossad did not yet know if the reactor was operational or not, but they had to find out. Judging from the 15-month-old images they acquired, they realized that construction of the nuclear reactor was probably in an advanced stage.

1ST PHASE:
THE INTEL
GATHERING MISSION

Since Mossad was not sure at what stage of completion the nuclear reactor was, they opted for a risky decision to send operatives in to check it out. This prompted them to call upon Israel's most elite black ops unit of *the Sayeret Matkal.*

Sayeret Matkal is the highest commando unit of the army of Israel. Their job is to complete special operations considered beyond the scope of regular troops. This unit has a model similar to that of the SAS (British), seal team, and delta force. The Sayeret Matkal is actually among the highest trained troops in the world.

This unit has a particular specialty-they operate covertly behind enemy lines. Generally, they silently infiltrate enemy countries and gather intelligence. The Sayeret Matkal has completed missions in Jordan and Lebanon, and has gone in and out of these countries without detection.

In mid-August 2007, selected Sayeret Matkal unit commandos prepared to set out on their mission: to confirm the existence of

Syria's nuclear program. 2 low-flying and almost silent helicopters were used to ferry 12 commandos to the site. Although unconfirmed, the commandos were probably wearing Syrian uniforms.

The helicopters dropped them off at a safe distance from the facility (around 1 mile away). This mission was a risky one because if compromised, there would be no way to rescue the unit. To compound the risk, if the unit made a mistake that led to their discovery or mission failure, it would undoubtedly lead the two countries to war.

When the unit was a few feet away from the facility, they immediately started gathering intelligence. They collected water and soil samples from around the facility. This was the most important part of their mission and was the only way Israel could be sure if the reactor was operational or not. But, how?

If the reactor were in an active state, small(non-lethal) portions of radioactive substances would deposit in the water and soil. After the commandos finished gathering the Intel, they hid their tracks and prepared to go back. However, before they could finish, Syrian soldiers appeared and almost caught them. Luckily, they managed to escape undetected and safely returned to Israel with the samples.

The samples underwent nuclear contamination testing at a Government lab in Tel Aviv. Dagan and Olmert later received the results; the results were positive. The samples contained traces of nuclear contamination. The traces were at levels that indicated that the nuclear reactor was not fully operational. The results meant Olmert could now give the order to take out the facility.

Anonymous sources reported that once the material gathered tested positive and confirmed to originate from Korea, the United States approved Israel's attack on the site. However, senior U.S officials later claimed they did not approve and were not involved in the attack, but had prior notice. In his memoir, the former president of the United States, President George W. Bush wrote, 'Decision Points' that Prime Minister of Israel, Ehud Olmert had requested the U.S to bomb the nuclear site in Syria but Bush refused. He said the intelligence gathered was not definitive enough to determine if the site was part of a nuclear weapons program.

Bush further claimed that Olmert did not ask for approval to attack and that he did not approve for an attack. He also stated that Olmert acted according to what he thought was necessary, what he needed to do to protect Israel.

Another report also indicated that Israel had planned to attack the Syrian nuclear site as early as 14 July, but some U.S officials, including Condoleezza Rice, then the Secretary of State, opted for a public condemnation of Syria, which only delayed the Israeli military attack until they feared the information would leak to the press.

The Israeli prime minister called his top intelligence and military chiefs to a meeting. During the meeting, they all agreed on one thing: *the nuclear reactor was intolerable and something they could not allow.*

The only available option to take out the reactor was through an airstrike simply because airpower has a number of advantages. For starters, it is a very speedy method easily used to engage and disengage before the enemy realizes what has happened.

The prime minister then issued an order to prepare for an air attack on the Syrian reactor and the meeting codenamed the operation operation orchard. For the operation to succeed, the prime minister had to work with another of Israel's top Special Forces unit, *squadron 69* also called *the hammer squadron.*

Squadron 69 was the best unit suited for this mission because they had successfully conducted a similar mission 25 years earlier where eight squadron 69 jets flew into Iranian airspace to bomb a nuclear facility Saddam Hussein was building. They managed to evade Iranian air defenses and take out the reactor in almost clin. ical strikes.

However, the attack on Syria was much harder to pull off because over time, Syria had developed one of the best anti-aircraft systems in the world. Luckily, squadron 69 acquired f-15 and f-16 fighter jets, aircrafts specifically designed to evade such systems. These fighter jets use ECM flairs against guided missiles. They also carry electronic countermeasures used to fool Air Defense Systems so they can infiltrate enemy airspace without detection.

General Eliezer Shkedi, commander of the Israeli Air force, personally handpicked the Israeli Air Force pilots who were to be in the operation. Shkedy chose pilots who had flying skills similar to his own. The pilots began training a few weeks before the raid.

Their training revolved around hitting small targets on the ground at an angled dive of about 35 degrees. During the practice missions, the pilots used fake bombs that exploded white phosphorous smoke. General Eliezer Shkedi used this to determine the accuracy of the drops. The drills happened at night, over the Negev.

On 3 September, around 3 days before the airstrike, the prime minister received more Intel that forced his hand. Mossad had detected activity at the Syrian coast: A 1700-tonne, north Korean ship had arrived at the Syrian port of Tartus. The ship was carrying materials that were labeled as cement.

As the ship was undergoing unloading, a Mossad agent used a hidden camera to photograph what was happening. Ronen Solomon, an Israeli on-line data analyst found a trace for the cargo ship named Al-Hamed. They determined that the docked ship was not carrying cement as indicated, but rather, the ship was ferrying materials to be used to complete the nuclear reactor and make it fully operational. This meant Olmert had no more time to waste. He had to act immediately.

On 4 September 2007, the key players involved in the mission met up at General Eliezer Shkedi headquarters. The focus of this meeting was the agent's report and the photographs taken by the Mossad agents as the Syrians unloaded the North Korean ship.

Some newspapers also reported that Ali Reza Asgari, an Iranian Brigadier General, had disappeared in February possibly deflecting to the west, had supplied Western intelligence with some information about the nuclear reactor site in Al-Kibar.

2ND PHASE:
BOMBING THE NUCLEAR
REACTOR MISSION

On 5 September 2007, at 11:59PM, 10 squadron 69 pilots were preparing to take off. During the preparation, they had not received any information about the nature of their mission, or their target. After they completed their preparation, the f-15 and f-16 took off from the Ramat David Airbase, 20 seconds apart. In their weapons arsenal were laser-guided 500-pound AGM 65 bombs.

The jets then headed out to sea at 600 miles per hour. They followed a route that would help them avoid Syrian air-defense systems, a root mapped out by the Israeli air force. They were to fly from Israel and over to the west, over the Mediterranean Sea, then North, then Eastwards, above the Syrian Turkish border, then over Turkish airspace.

Back in Israel, the prime minister and senior military commanders gathered at the pit, an Israeli Air Force underground command center in Tel Aviv. From this point, they were to monitor the route followed by the fighter jets. After establishing that the jets had no technical faults, they ordered three f-15 jets to return to base. The remaining seven jets continued on the planned route at low altitudes.

At this point, General Shkedi briefed the pilots about the target. He told the pilots they were flying into heavily defended Syrian airspace. He also assured them that the Syrian air-defense systems would be jammed. He also warned them to avoid dropping bombs on civilians. Fighter jets pilots undergo intense training aimed at helping them suppress their nerves to avoid the feeling of fear.

A few minutes later, the jets were over Syrian airspace. Using jamming, electronic attack, and conventional precision bombs, they destroyed a Syrian radar site located in Tall al-Abyad area. They also used codes, allegedly sold to them by Russians, to trick the Syrian air-defense systems into displaying hundreds of enemy aircrafts for a slight moment, and then detect no planes.

The radar screens on the Syrian system showed normal skies. Israel did this to make the Syrians think their radar system was experiencing a slight technical problem. The technology used to neutralize the radars might have been similar to the Suter airborne network attack system. This would make it possible to manipulate enemy sensors directly or feed the enemy's radar emitters with false targets.

The prime minister and senior military commanders then sent the precise co-ordinates of the al-Kibar nuclear reactor to the Israeli pilots' onboard computers and the planes swung southwards to begin their bombing route.

Generally, this is the riskiest part of the mission, when they finally get to their target. This is their most vulnerable point because the pilots are not defending themselves, they are aiming at the target. As the pilots were about to bomb their target, they suddenly detected anti-aircraft rockets. Back in the pit, they had no idea what was going on but feared the worst. They did not know if the Syrian had detected and shot down their fighter jets, or if the mission was a success.

Finally, a radio transmission came through with the word 'Arizona', the code word chosen to confirm the bombs had hit their target. Not a single Israeli fighter jet was lost and the nuclear reactor was nothing more than a smoking ruin. The most dangerous part of the mission was over.

The pilots then exited Syrian airspace at high speeds having successfully completed their mission. Olmert immediately called the Whitehouse to inform President George Bush of the mission's success.

After The Reactor Bombing

After the bombing, there was a tense wait to see how Syria would respond. Olmert was confident Syria would not react publicly, but he could not be certain. Immediately after the raid, he sent a message to the president of Syria, Bashar al-Assad saying Israel would not openly take credit for the raid.

This gamble paid off; the Syrian state news announced their military had successfully repelled Israeli planes from Syrian airspace. Although this was a lie, both countries were content with pretending the bombing had not happened.

With this, it seemed as if Olmert had successfully safeguarded the future of Israel. However, one thing still bothered Prime Minister Olmert and Dagan: how Syria had managed to develop a nuclear weapons program in complete secrecy. For seven years, Israel had not known that Syria was building a nuclear reactor.

Generally, a nuclear reactor is not something easily hidden because it is a huge facility. This prompted Mossad to investigate how Syria had managed to keep the al-Kibar nuclear facility a secret.

Mossad investigators discovered that the Syrians had developed a networking system that helped them avoid all electronic communications. They decided to go back in time and use 'snail mail' to avoid sending sensitive information over electronic transmission that enemy combatants could easily intercept or tap into.

Every time they needed to send a message, they would print a hard copy, place it in an envelope, seal it with wax in an envelope, write top secret, and send it just like it was done in the old days. However, they had to build their own network of couriers that would transport the envelopes from place to place.

At the center of that communication system, was a man renowned for his hatred of Israel and one of the most powerful people in Syria: General Muhammad Suleiman. General Muhammad Suleiman was also an advisor to the president. His office was located just across the hall from the president's office in the presidential palace in Damascus.

Mossad discovered he was the mastermind behind Syria's top secret nuclear program. He had gotten credit for the compartmentalization within Syria's government. They allowed him to undertake the project for years without anyone knowing of it.

With the dawn of the new Intel, Mossad uncovered information that was even more worrying. The raid done on the al-Kibar reactor did not shake General Suleiman. After the bombing of the nuclear reactor, more Intel showed that Syria was resuming its efforts to build another nuclear facility.

The Syrians would have started from scratch, but with General Suleiman in charge, it seemed that the nuclear weapons program would soon be running again. Generally, Syria already had the knowhow, it had money, and the determination to do it. Having all these, it would only take them five years to have an operation ally ready nuclear bomb.

Mossad was convinced that as long as General Suleiman remained in charge, the threat of a nuclear bombing remained. At this point, the only option Israel could come up with was to take out the threat to assassinate General Suleiman.

3RD PHASE:
THE ELIMINATING THREAT
CONTINUITY MISSION

Eliminating General Suleiman proved a much harder task than bombing the nuclear reactor. The reactor was just a static building. However, the General was a cautious man. All his movements were a closely guarded secret known to only a few people. In Damascus, he was under armed guards. Eliminating him there would be impossible for the Mossad.

In summer 2008, Mossad received Intel that General Suleiman was planning to spend a weekend at his second home, a villa in the coastal city of Tartus. Security in this area was far more relaxed than in Damascus. If Mossad wanted to ensure the assassinating of the General was to be successful, Tartus was the best place and time to do it.

The mission would require another of Israel's black ops units - The Kidon, the unit known for assassinations and the most secretive of all of Israeli elite units. The Israeli government or the Israeli media has never released the operational details of any of their missions.

As the Kidon unit was studying the General's villa, they noticed that although it was a well-guarded fortress, from the sea, the rear of the villa remained totally exposed. They also discovered that when General Suleiman was at his villa, he hosted his guests at the balcony that overlooked the sea.

Initially, the Kidon unit considered the option of bringing a boat close enough to the shore for a sniper to target the General from the boat. However, officials vetoed this plan; they had only one chance to eliminate him and a long shot from a boat would be risky. Generally, the further the sniper is from the target, the harder it is for him to get a headshot. At this point, the only other option available was to send someone onto the shore.

On 2 August 2008, a yacht sailed on the Mediterranean coast towards Tartus. The yacht's registration showed it belonged to a wealthy businessman; however, on this day, it was ferrying two Kidon snipers. About a mile off the coast, the yacht dropped its sails and the two assassins made their way to the shore. At the same time, the General arrived at his home in readiness for the weekend stay.

As the sun went down, the snipers emerged from the water. They watched the General's guests as they mingled on the terrace. Eventually, the General appeared to have dinner with his family and friends who sat around the table. As the General was entertaining the guests, both the snipers lined him up in their crosshairs and prepared to take the shot.

Suddenly, one of the guests obscured the General. This forced them to move to a new position where they would get a clear shot of the target. They then aimed their rifles. Both snipers wore earpieces that helped them hear an electronic countdown. The countdown intention was to ensure they fired simultaneously. When the countdown ran out, they took the shot. Both bullets found a target: One in the neck and one in the head. The snipers then escaped without detection.

Just as they did after the airstrike that destroyed Syria's nuclear reactor, Israel did not admit to the assassination of General Suleiman; instead, they referred to it as a 'very happy accident'

Later, Iranian media reported that a silenced weapon was the weapon used to gun down General Suleiman. A Mossad spy arrested sometime after the assassination testified to scouting certain points where General Suleiman assassination happened.

Other reports by Wiki leaks showed that France told us that General Suleiman's assassination was probably due to rivalries in the Government of Syria. They claimed that Maher al-Assad, brother to the President of Syria, had probably ordered the killing. France also added that a sniper did not assassinate General Suleiman while he was at his coastal home, but that he the General was gunned down in his car.

However, in 2015, a National Security Agency document leaked by Edward Snowden, a former NSA agent showed that Israel's Naval Commandos were responsible for the assassination. This was the first official confirmation that General Suleiman's assassination was an operation conducted by the Israeli military.

Snowden's leak ended speculation that the murder of General Suleiman bred from disputes within the government of Syria. The information contained in the NSA document had the labeling 'si' to mean the intelligence gathered was from intercepted communication signals.

General Suleiman was buried on 3 August 2008 at his home village in Draykish/Duraykish, which is located 15 miles East of Tartus. Maher al-Assad, President Bashar al-Assad's younger brother, participated in the funeral. He seemed very upset about the murder.

However, as investigations into the murder were ongoing, Syrian authorities discovered approximately $80 million US dollars in cash hidden in the basement of General Suleiman's home. Reports said that this finding greatly unsettled President al-Assad, who ended up launching investigations into how General Suleiman had managed to obtain such huge amounts of money.

Assad feared that General Suleiman had betrayed him. It remained unclear whether the general had siphoned the money to fund Tehran or just for his personal use.

Israel's assassination of General Suleiman raised many questions about whether Israel had violated international laws as they conducted the operation or the main purpose of the killing.

Hassan Nasrallah, leader of Hezbollah, told journalists that the Israeli government conducted the killing. He claimed that the assassination connected to the role General Suleiman played in the war between Hezbollah and Israel in July 2006.

But even after the assassination of General Suleiman, one thing that still boggled people's mind was how Syria managed to keep the reactor a secret. Let us look at this closely in the following chapter.

HOW SYRIA HAD MANAGED TO KEEP THE REACTOR A SECRET

For starters, the nuclear reactor facility was in a very remote desert area. This area was strategic because there was a low probability of people movement near the facility.

The Syrians also built the facility in a canyon that concealed it from view. This meant it was at a lower level than the surrounding land, thus hidden to people traveling on ground. The Syrians took further measures to conceal the facility by adding earth, wall, or mound placed on low-lying land to block the facility view on the canyon. All these features made the facility visible only from above.

The site also lacked any over defensive features such as a tight security fence that would have drawn attention. They also concealed the facility from spies that may have tried to investigate it from the sky.

The Syrians fitted the building with a roof even before they completed building the building. They built the walls in a way that altered its shape when viewed from above. The Syrian engineers that worked on the building also went to extraordinary lengths to hide the ventilation and power lines, cooling systems, and other features that are the most identifiable signs of a nuclear reactor.

From the sky, the main building appeared shallow and small. However, the facility had large underground chambers that were tens of meters deep. The chambers were large enough to house a reserve water-storage tank, pools for the spent fuel rods, as well as the reactor itself. The facility also had an extensive network of electrical power lines that were buried in trenches that stretched across the terrain.

The Syrian engineers building this facility had also replaced traditional water-cooling systems found in other reactors with an underground system that discharged waste into the Euphrates River.

As for the ventilation towers that look like smokestacks, a common feature in most nuclear reactor sites, the ventilation system used on the Al-Kibar site was along the walls of the building. They had louver openings not visible from the air. In light of these findings, experts determined that international and domestic capabilities of detecting such nuclear plants would prove difficult in the near future.

SYRIA HIDES EVIDENCE
OF THE ISRAELI ATTACK

By early October 2007, Syria had begun dismantling the remains of the site bombed by the Israeli. U.S and other foreign officials familiar with the site said this was Syria's attempt to prevent international scrutiny of the location/site.

From evidence collected from overhead photography, the officials said that the al-Kibar site had characteristics (signature) of a rather small but substantial nuclear reactor similar to one in North Korea.

Syria's disassembly of the site sought to serve the purpose of making it difficult for weapons inspectors from the global nuclear watchdog, the International Atomic Energy agency (IAEA), to determine the true nature of the facility or determine how Syria intended to use it.

After the raid, Syria displayed photos to journalists to back their claims that Israel had bombed an empty building. However, anonymous officials said the bombed site was a lot more different from the one shown to the journalists.

Before the Israeli attack, satellite images showed a tall and boxlike building under construction. After the raid, the box-like building was still there but destroyed. However, Commercial satellite images taken later by a Digitalglobe satellite showed bulldozers or tractors and scrape marks on the area where the building once stood. Syria had done its best to wipe clean the suspected site of the nuclear site.

The new photos depicted the same site in earlier images, but the building had vanished and now replaced by dirt. The trucks and construction equipment seen in earlier images had also vanished. The only structure still visible in the new images was a small additional building that stood on the riverbank approximately 600 yards from the main building.

Nuclear experts reported that the small building might have been a pumping station used to supply water to the nuclear reactors.

After the demolition, Syria subsequently erected a light metal frame building over the site of the destroyed facility and began preparing a pipeline to connect the water pumping system on the site to a water treatment plant a few kilometers away in an attempt to further cover-up the nuclear nature of the site. The purpose of the new building was probably to use it as a ruse to excavate previously irremovable debris of the reactor.

Other countries, including Iran in 2003 and 2004 and Iraq after the war in the Persian Gulf, have also tried this approach of hiding nuclear evidence. Iraq and Iran bulldozed buildings suspected to be nuclear reactors.

David Albright, the president of the Institute for Science and International security, said that Syria cleared and dismantled the facility in a very quick manner that makes it look like they were trying to hide something suspicious. Generally, the reaction was quicker than would be expected given the fact that the IAEA wanted to visit the site.

Albright said that the swift move Syria took was because the Israeli attack had blown a hole on the roof of the building, which would have exposed everything housed inside to satellites and spy aircrafts. If the Syrians had not cleared the building, then from its construction, inspectors would have known that its purpose was to house an North Korean-modeled reactor.

IAEA INVESTIGATIONS

Syria's action to cover up the airstrike only added fears that Syria was secretly trying to build a nuclear reactor. This kind of work would have been against the rules of the Nuclear Non-Proliferation Treaty that Syria was signatory to.

Under the treaty, Syria had an obligation to inform the International Atomic Energy Agency of the decision to construct a nuclear facility. Syria signed the agreement back in 1992 and was therefore obligated to abide by it and report its nuclear developments and plans to the IAEA.

If the Atomic Agency determined that Syria was in violation of its responsibilities, it would refer the issue to the United Nations Security council for sanctions, as had been the case with Iran.

After the destruction of the nuclear reactor, IAEA requested to inspect the alleged nuclear site.

However, Syria rejected the request, claiming that the installation at al-Kibar was a non-nuclear military facility the IAEA had no right to access. However, in June 2008, under international pressure, Syria allowed a team of IAEA inspectors to visit the site.

At the site, inspectors managed to uncover evidence of undeclared nuclear material. They also assessed that the containment structure, water pumping system, and the overall size of the building could have been sufficient for a nuclear reactor.

The IAEA also noticed access to three other sites related to the alKibar nuclear site, areas also suspected to relate to a covert nu. clear program. However, Syria continued denying the findings.

On June 9, 2011, the IAEA found Syria in violation of the agreements and reported it to the United Nations Security Council.

After the 2011 onset of civil war in Syria, a number of sites throughout the country have fallen under the control of rebels. In February 2013, the free army took over the al-Kibar site. Video footage released documented the state of the site. According to the video, the new building was in use as a stationery launch site for scud missiles.

Syrian residents living in villages near the destroyed Al-Kibar nuclear site (about 60 Kilometers from Deir A Zor) reported that members of the Daesh/ISIS (Islamic State) had been excavating the site. In 2014, ISIS had taken over the site from the Syrian rebels. Some residents who visited the area also reported seeing empty metal barrels; this further increased fears that radioactive materials were still present there.

The Islamic State may have been searching for radioactive materials that they could use to make a bomb.

SYRIA STILL PUSHING FOR NUCLEAR WEAPONS

After Israel's airstrike on the al-Kibar nuclear reactor, the belief was that Israel had managed to destroy all of Syria's nuclear weapon capability. However, new information suggests that Bashar al-Assad was still in pursuit of building another nuclear bomb. Western intelligence suggested that the Syrian government was in the process of constructing a new secret nuclear plant aimed at nuclear weapon production.

In late 2008, the Israeli government told the IAEA that Syria had once again been 'actively involved in the production of plutonium' and that Damascus had renewed its collaboration with North Korea for Nuclear arms. They also claimed that North Korea was actively supplying research and nuclear materials to Syria.

A report posted in a Germany leading magazine, Del Spiegel, claimed that the Syrian government had transported 8,000 fuel rods at the al-Kibar site before the bombing to a new location in the western part of the country. The report cited this information from 'western intelligence sources', sources it did not disclose.

The magazine also claimed it had seen intelligence reports that contained transcriptions of intercepted radio traffic and satellite photographs. This left little doubt that the government of Syria was indeed in the process of creating a new nuclear reactor.

The magazine further reported that the plant was under construction in a remote and mountainous region; deep underground near Al-Quasar, a small town located less than 2 miles from the Northern border of Lebanon.

The construction of the site, something the Syrians codenamed Zamzam' began in 2009 under the watchful eye of Hezbollah, a Lebanese paramilitary group. The belief was that Hezbollah was using 'elite units' to man the new plant.

The site appeared to be in an ideal location because it connected to the power grid via special access nodes connected to Blosah, a nearby city. Another suspicious detail about the facility is that it is also considerably adjacent to water supplies. The facility has a connection to Lake Zaita, which is four Kilometers away. This kind of a connection is not necessary for a normal weapons depot, but is vital for a nuclear facility.

The radio traffic intercepted included conversations between the head of Syrian Atomic Energy Commission, Ibrahim Othman, and Senior Syrian Military Officials. The conversations seemed to point out that Iranian Guard Corps members were aiding the construction of the site. The article in the German magazine also showed that Western intelligence was sure North Korean experts were heading the technical aspects of the new site - where some of them are still in Damascus.

According to the IAEA, the government of Syria had approximately 50 tons of uranium. If it were to be enriched, then it would provide material to build up to 3-5 nuclear bombs.

The Institute for Science and International Security based in Washington DC also indicated the probability of there being such large amounts of uranium in Syria and in 2013, expressed its concern.

They said that the large stock of natural uranium would pose nuclear proliferation risks. What is worse is that it would be very risky if dangerous organizations such as the Al-Qaida, the Hezbollah, or some of States like Iran that have undeclared nuclear programs such as Iran obtained the uranium. Some of the uranium remained hidden for some time at Marj al-Sultan, a location near Damascus. The IAEA has pinpointed this area as a suspicious point.

Satellite images from December 2012-February 2013 show suspicious activity around the area. The area was a point of heavy rebel fights despite its closeness to a Syrian army base. This meant the rebels were willing to risk war to obtain something special from the site.

However, with help from Hezbollah as well as armed militia, the government troops acted fast and moved everything from the site to the Al-Quasar site. Eventually, Marj al-Sultan fell under rebel control but government forces later re-captured it. After ignoring it thinking it was a conventional weapons depot for Hezbollah, experts have now been keeping a close eye on AlQuasar.

34

From the beginning, Syria has been doing a good job of disguising the new nuclear site. They dumped the excavated sand at different locations to make it hard for anyone to know the facility's depth. Further, the military heavily guarded the entrances to the facility as a precautionary measure previously lacking on the alKibar site.

In the spring of 2013, the areas around Al-Quasar area experienced heavy fighting but the area around the site remained untouched, However many of Hezbollah's elite units stationed there died.

The most recent satellite images of the site shows six structures built on the ground; the structures include one guardhouse and five sheds. Three of the sheds are believed to conceal entrances to the underground facility.

Further proof that makes the site suspicious is the amount of radio traffic that was recently intercepted by spies. A voice identified as one of the high-ranking Hezbollah members was heard quoting an 'atomic factory' and kept mentioning Al-Quasar. It is evident that the man speaking is familiar with the site. The radio traffic also showed the man had communications with Ibrahim Othman, the head of Syrian Atomic Energy Commission.

The Hezbollah man speaking is also heard using the codename for the site, 'Zamzam' - which is a traditional Muslim word for the well God created in the desert for the second wife of Abraham, Hagar, and her son, Ishmael.

The conversations intercepted also mention the work done by members of Iran's Revolutionary Guard. The Revolutionary Guard is generally a paramilitary organization that works under direct orders of the supreme leader of Iran, Ali Khamenei.

This organization controls part of the economy of Iran and has a key role in Iran's nuclear activities. Most of its work outside the country lacks government clearance. This organization can be termed as a state within a state.

Experts also suggest that North Korea is still involved with the AlQuasar nuclear project. On the al-Kibar facility bombed by Israel, Ibrahim Othman worked closely with Chou Ji Bu who was the en gineer in charge of the Yongbyon Reactor in North Korea.

After the al-Kibar facility incident, intelligence reports believed Chou to have disappeared. Western intelligence experts claim he hid in Damascus and continued working with Othman. Experts believe that the new Al-Quasar facility would have been impossible to build without the knowledge of North Koreans. The workmanship done on the fuel rods also depicts the involvement of North Korea.

ISRAEL ADMITS TO THE SYRIAN STRIKE AS A WARNING FOR IRAN

After revelations that Iran was also planning to build a nuclear reactor, an Israeli cabinet minister broke Israel's secrecy policy after he admitted to the Syria airstrike on the Al-Kibar reactor. He used the admittance as a pretext to strike Iran without the support of the United States. Before this, Israel had never officially admitted to the strike despite former US President George Bush writing about it in his Memoirs.

This served as a threat to Iran that Israel would not hesitate to at tack if they found out that they were building a nuclear bomb. The government of Prime Minister Netanyahu made it very clear that they were prepared to attack unilaterally if it deemed necessary in spite of calls to give diplomacy a chance and divided domestic opinion.

The then United States secretary of state, Hillary Clinton had stated that negotiations and sanctions were the best approach for Iran's case. However, Prime Minister Netanyahu said that if nobody drew a 'red line' for Iran, then it would continue pursuing the need to create an atomic bomb.

The prime minister also said that each passing day brings Tran closer to nuclear bombs. He also added that the world tells Israel to wait. He said that countries in the international community, who are not willing to draw a red line before Iran, do not have a moral right to draw a red line before Israel. This sent a clear message that no country should stop Israel from attacking Iran.

The pentagon ran a declassified war simulation that forecasted that such a strike on Iran would only lead to a wider regional war that could include the US. This simulation also indicated about 200 Americans would die and there would be heavy Israeli and Iranian casualties as Iran retaliated. Hezbollah, backed by Iran, recently vowed to attack Israel if they were to strike Iran.

Mike Mullen, a US admiral, said that the United States was aware that a military strike on Iran would destabilize the whole of the Middle East region. It may also generate a race for nuclear weapons in that region.

Prime Minister Netanyahu also swore that he would ensure Tehran would not obtain nuclear weapons. Iran, however, signed a United Nations agreement to dismantle, albeit partially, their nuclear infrastructure in what was referred to as 'implementation day'.

Israel's prime minister however warned that he would make his defenses stronger, increase his intelligence resources and warned of dire consequences should Iran violate the deal.

ASSASSINATION OF IRANIAN NUCLEAR SCIENTISTS

Between 2010 and 2012, four Iranian nuclear scientists were murdered. One more scientist escaped with wounds after an attempted assassination. Two of the murders were planned using magnetic bombs attached to the target's cars.

On 15 January 2007, Iranian authorities reported Ardeshir Hosseinpour, an Iranian junior scientist, assistant professor, and authority on electromagnetism had died of gas poisoning due to a faulty heater. However, these claims were reported to have been foul play.

According to reports by Stratfor, a private intelligence firm, Mossad poisoned the Iranian nuclear scientist through radiation poisoning. However, Iranian officials denied this claim saying their scientists were safe.

Later in 2014, Mahboobeh, sister to the dead scientist, accused the Iranian Revolutionary Guard of Iran for being behind the killing, She claimed they had murdered her brother because he had refused to work on Iraq's nuclear enrichment program.

On July 23, 2011, gunmen on a motorcycle gunned and killed Darioush Rezaeinejad, an Iranian engineering student, as he, his wife, and 5-year-old daughter were returning home.

On 12 January 2010, a motorcycle bomb explosion in North Tehran killed Masoud Alimohammadi, a quantum field theorist, elementary-particle physicist, and a professor of elementary particle physics at the University of Tehran's Department of Physics.

Reports indicated he was on his way to work when a motorcycle parked close to his car exploded.

On 29 November 2010 in Northern Tehran, an unidentified person on a motorcycle used a magnetic bomb attaché to murder Majid Shahriari, a nuclear engineer who worked with the Atomic Energy Organization of Iran. In the attack, Majid Shahriari's wife sustained injuries.

On 29 November 2010, someone attempted to assassinate Fereydoon Abbasi-Davani, another nuclear scientist, using the same technique used to assassinate Majid Shahriari. However, Abbasi exited the vehicle before the magnetic bomb exploded. During the attempted assassination, both he and his wife sustained injuries.

On January 11 2012, Mostafa Ahmadi Roshan, an Iranian nuclear scientist was assassinated near Gol Nabi Street in North Tehran using an electric bomb attached to his vehicle. His driver later died in hospital after sustaining fatal injuries after the explosion.

On 14 January 2012, Iran sent a message to the U.S government via the Swiss embassy in Tehran saying it had evidence that directly linked the CIA to the murder of Mostafa. As a response to this assassination, Israeli army speaker said they did not shed a tear for the murder.

Before the murder of Mostafa, the commando of the Israeli army said that 2012 would be a critical year for Iran that would be full of un-normal events. Following his death, the Natanz Nuclear facility was later renamed in honor of Mostafa.

The government of Iran accused Israel for the murders. From 2011-2012, Iranian authorities arrested a few Iranians claiming they had carried out the murders on behalf of Israel's intelligence service, Mossad.

U.S officials and Western intelligence are said to have confirmed Israel's connection to the murders. In June 2012, the government of Israel was confident that it arrested the assassins.

The Iranian government had blamed both the United States and Israel for the assassinations. The American secretary of state at that time, Hillary Clinton, categorically denied that the U.S had any role in the assassinations.

In early 2011, Majid Jamali Fashi, a young Iranian, confessed to the murder of Masoud Alimohammadi on Iranian state TV. He claimed he had undergone training for the mission in a Mossad facility that is near Tel Aviv. In May 2012, Majid was executed.

Still in May. Iranian authorities announced they had arrested 14 more Iranians, who were said to have carried out five of the attacks on the Iranian nuclear scientists. Iran claimed Israel had trained them. Iran's channel 1 (IRTV) broadcasted a 1/2 hour documentary named Terror Club; the documentary featured televised confessions of 12 of the arrested suspects.

According to Time Magazine, Western Intelligence confirmed that Iranian intelligence cracked two espionage rings backed by Mossad. It was said that Mossad officials were shocked and pissed to see their assets paraded on Iranian TV.

The magazine also stated that in 2012, Iran had attempted to retaliate against Israel for the murder of their nuclear scientists by launching about 20 hastily organized attacks. The attacks targeted Israel's diplomatic missions across the globe. However, none of them were successful.

Israel has never denied nor confirmed their involvement in the murders. However, Moshe Ya'alon, former Chief of Staff of the Israel Defense Forces, and former Israel's defense minister stated that Israel would act in any way, and was not willing to tolerate Iran's nuclear arms. He however ended by saying that they preferred Iran nuclear disarmament to happen through sanctions.

The assassination spree ended in 2013 following pressure from diplomats in the US. At the time, the US was trying to reach an agreement with Iran on restrictions on its nuclear activity, Mossad officials are also reported to have concluded that these attacks were generally 'too dangerous' for their valued intelligence agents in Iran.

Since then, reports indicated Mossad had informed its spy network in Iran to concentrate on collecting any evidence of breach of agreement; evidence Israel can use to further restrict Iran nuclear activity.

In January 2015, Iranian authorities claimed they had thwarted another Mossad attempt to assassinate another nuclear scientist.

Why Israel Cannot Just Attack Iran?

Iran's nuclear knowledge remains concentrated in the minds of a few scientists. Israel's assassination of these scientists creates a major setback to their national nuclear program. The murders also scare the talent out of the business of nuclear science because the Iranian government would not tolerate the assassinations.

From Iran's point of view, Israel also bears the blame for the killings because it does not want to bear the blame for starting a war. If Israel were to bomb the nuclear reactor itself, and a war between the two countries erupted, Israel would bear the blame for starting it.

Once such a war starts, the United States would also find itself drawn into the war. Israel's preference is that America bombs the Iranian nuclear facilities mainly because the US has better strike capabilities. If Israel was to launch strikes on Iran while the US still considers a diplomatic approach the best approach, then Israel could not count on the U.S to help, which is perhaps why the US Constantly pushes Israel to stop assassinating Iranian nuclear scientists.

OTHER ISRAEL
STRIKES IN SYRIA

January 2013

The Syrian military reported Israeli jets conducted an airstrike on a military research center in the North Western area of Damascus.

July 2013

US officials reported that the Israeli air force hit a missile warehouse in the Latika area.

3 and 5 May 2013 (The Rif Dimashq Airstrikes)

These series of airstrikes were directed at specific targets. The attack on 3 May targeted a warehouse at Damascus International Airport. The warehouse housed surface-to-surface missiles acquired from Iran. The missiles were bound for Hezbollah in Lebanon. The bombed warehouse was under the control of Iran's Quds Force and the Hezbollah.

Anonymous sources claimed the missiles were probably Fateh-110's and included Scud-D missiles. After the airstrike, satellite images showed that the two-bombed facilities on opposite sides of the airport were completely destroyed.

SANA, a Syrian State News Agency reported the attacks conducted on 5 May were at the North Eastern part of Jamraya, Al-Dimas Ai base and Maysalun (Damascus countryside on the border with Lebanon). Syria claimed the attack was with rockets.

Israel never denied nor confirmed their involvement. Syrians denied ever being an attack on 3 May but accused Israel of the 5 May attacks.

Casualties from the two attacks included more than 42 dead soldiers and many civilian casualties.

THE CURRENT
SITUATION IN SYRIA

Earlier in 2016, there were around 50 nuclear bombs stored in an air base in Turkey, which is about 110 Kilometers (70 miles) from the border of Syria. There was speculation that terrorists or other hostile groups could steal the nuclear weapons.

According to the Obama administration, Assad must step down so that Syria can get back to a state of peace. According to the Obama administration, everything going on in Syria, from the Civil war, to ISIL, to nuclear activity points towards al-Assad's poor administration.

President Obama said the war in Syria would not end with Bashar al-Assad still in power. However, Moscow supported President al Assad saying that Syria would collapse if al-Assad were to lose (or be removed) from power.

John Kerry, the American secretary of state warned the Syrian President that the US would adopt a new approach if he did not accept a political transition. In one of her presidential campaigns, Hillary Clinton also said she would review the strategy the US is using on Syria against the ISIS and the murderous regime of President Bashar al-Assad.

The conflict in Syria has led to the death of 470,000 Syrians and seen the displacement of about 1/22 of the country's population, approximately 23 million people, beyond and within the country.

Assad constantly abuses human rights to a very bad extent. He has turned weapons on his citizenry and hired mercenaries to murder in an effort meant to discourage dissent. ISIS has expanded in the manner it has only because Assad pulled his troops away from the border to re-enforce his despotic rule.

Hillary Clinton, the nominee of the Democratic Party for President of the United States in the 2016 election said she aimed to make this one of her first priorities if the United States citizenry elect her their president.

CONCLUSION

Thank you again for buying this book!

I hope this book was able to help you to learn more about Israel and Syria enmity, how it came to being, the Operation Orchard, as well as many other attacks carried out by Israel on Syria. To learn more, you would need to go a step further and read more about Israel and Syria relations and you will definitely uncover more interesting and intriguing information.

Finally, if you enjoyed this book, would you be kind enough to leave a review for this book on Amazon?

Please give me a great review for this book on Amazon!

Thank you and good luck!

Printed in Great Britain
by Amazon

34765100R00037